SCHUBERT

SONATA IN A MAJOR

OPUS 120, D. 664
FOR THE PIANO

EDITED BY MAURICE HINSON

AN ALFRED MASTERWORK EDITION

Copyright © MMVII by Alfred Publishing Co., Inc.
All rights reserved. Printed in USA.
ISBN-10: 0-7390-4538-5
ISBN-13: 978-0-7390-4538-1

Cover art: A Schubert Evening in a Viennese Home, *1897*
by Julius Schmid (1854–1935)
Oil on Canvas
Erich Lessing/Archiv für Kunst und Geschichte, London

Music Engraving and Interior: Bruce Nelson

FRANZ SCHUBERT
SONATA IN A MAJOR, OPUS 120, D. 664

Edited by Maurice Hinson

Foreword

The autograph for this sonata is lost, and therefore this edition is based on the *Sonaten für Pianoforte*, originally published by Breitkopf and Härtel, Leipzig, in 1888 as Series 10 of *Franz Schubert's Werke, Kritisch durchgesehene Gesammtausgabe*. Two other respected editions were examined when decisions were made regarding ornamentation and inconsistencies found in the 1888 edition listed above. These two other editions are *Franz Schubert Klaviersonaten*, Vol. I, edited by Paul Mies, Henle, 1971, and *Schubert Complete Pianoforte Sonatas*, Vol. II, edited by Howard Ferguson, The Associated Board of the Royal Schools of Music, 1980. The catalogue number "D. 664" refers to Otto Erich Deutsch's *Franz Schubert Thematisches Verzeichnis seine Werke in chronologiacher Folge*, published by Bärenreiter in 1978.

The problems that arise in trying to distinguish between various staccato marks (dot, dash or wedge) have led this editor to use only the dot to represent all three symbols. All pedal markings, fingerings and parenthetical material are editorial.

About the Music

Franz Schubert (1797–1828) was equally at home writing piano, vocal and chamber music. His unique style is characterized by great lyric beauty coupled with a bold harmonic vocabulary.

This sonata was written for the young pianist Josefine von Köhler during the summer of 1819, and features warm melodies and charming harmonies. There are numerous widely spaced chords in this work that must be arpeggiated. When these chords appear in the right hand, begin them *on* the beat and bring out the melody note. When the chords appear in the left hand, begin them slightly *before* the beat, and make the final note fall *on* the beat.

Allegro moderato 4

Form: Sonata-allegro.

Exposition: measures 1–47 (theme I = 1–20, theme II = 21–47); Development: 47–79; Recapitulation: 79–126 (theme I = 79–99, theme II = 100–126); Coda: 127–133.

In the opening measures, be sure that the melody flows naturally. Watch for quick mood changes, such as those in measures 8–9, 12–13, 33–34, 45–46, 56–57, etc. The octaves at measure 57 forward should not be played staccato; use as much finger legato as possible. Overall, this movement should be played at a leisurely pace throughout.

This edition is dedicated to Dr. Kent Lyman, with admiration and appreciation.

Maurice Hinson

Form: Tripartite.

Part I: measures 1–32 (A = 1–14, transition = 15, B = 16–32); Part II: 33–49. Part III: 50–70 (A = 50–59, B = 60–70); Coda: 71–75.

The form of this movement is constructed around variations of the simple theme stated in measures 1–7. In measure 10, take a little more time on the C-sharp. In measures 16, 18, 60 and 62 use finger pedal in the left hand by holding the first sixteenth note of each group of four. The climax of the movement is in measures 42–43. Then gradually diminish from measures 44–49.

Form: Sonata-allegro

Exposition: measures 1–84 (theme I = 1–18, theme II = 19–34, theme III = 35–84); Development: 84–121; Recapitulation: 121–205 (theme I = 121–139, theme II = 140–155, theme III = 156–205); Coda: 205–216.

Notice that the recapitulation (measure 121) begins in the subdominant, not the usual tonic. This is a device that Schubert used often. This movement has a dance-like character. Feel the meter as one beat per measure instead of two.

Sources Consulted in Preparation of This Edition

Butt, John. *Playing with History*. Cambridge, UK. Cambridge University Press, 2002.

Einstein, Alfred. *Schubert*. London: Cassell & Company, Ltd., 1951.

Hinson, Maurice. *Guide to the Pianist's Repertoire*, 3rd edition. Bloomington: Indiana University Press, 2000.

Luethi, F. E. *Schubert Solo Piano Literature*. Boulder, CO: Maxwell Music Evaluation, 1986.

Nagy, Christine. "Master Class with John Browning." *Clavier*, 20 (January 1981): 24-25.

Acknowledgements

Thanks to E. L. Lancaster and Carol Matz for their generous assistance and expert editorial advice, and to Angela C. Starnes for her superb administrative assistance.

Sonata in A Major

Franz Schubert (1797–1828)
Op. 120, D. 664

Allegro moderato (♩ = ca.108)

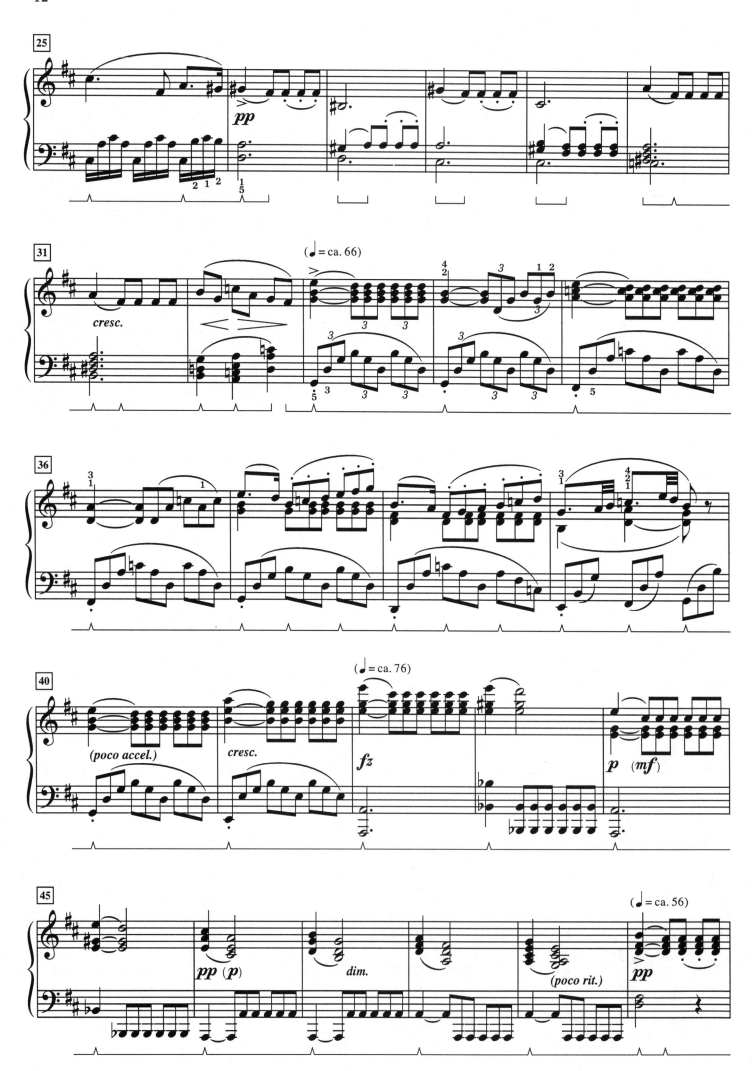

14

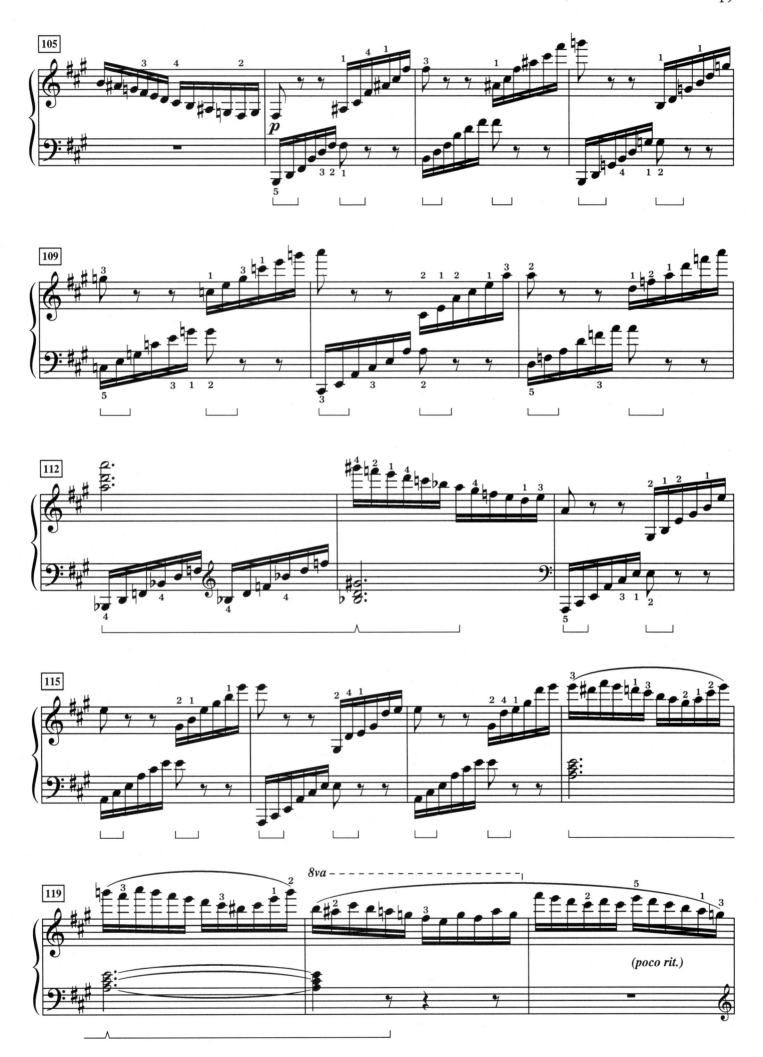

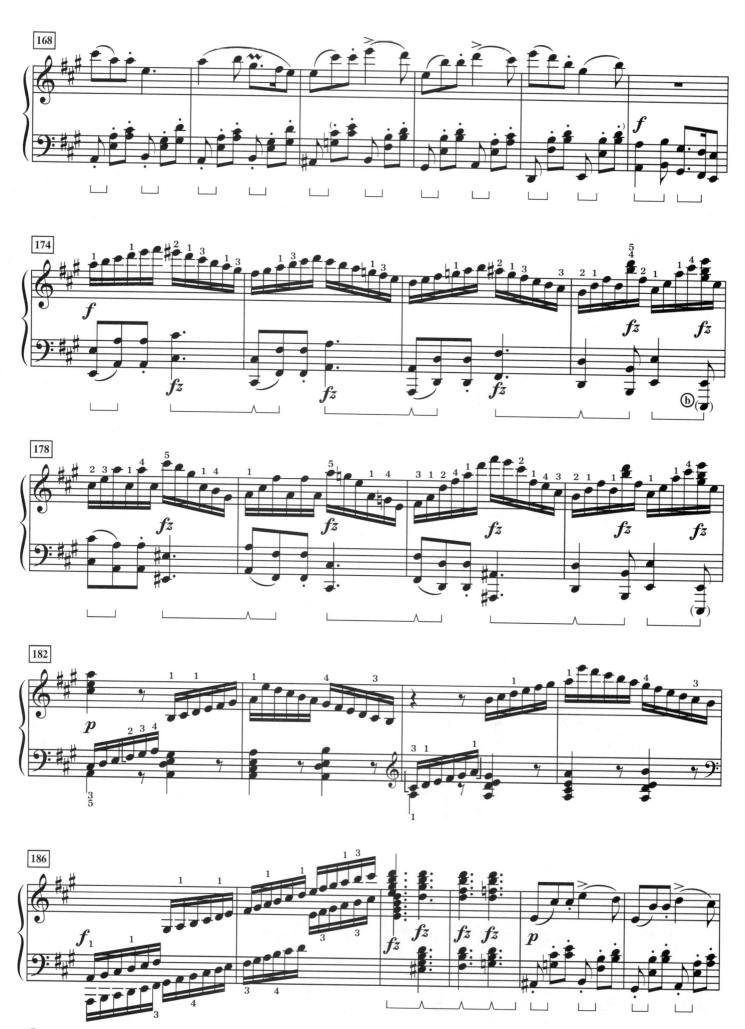

ⓑ This low E (also appearing in measure 181) was beyond the limitation of Schubert's piano, but it seems wise to play it on today's instruments.